Prayer Warrior:

A man's guide to an effective and powerful prayer life

Dr. Mike Edwards

Prayer Warrior: *A man's guide to an effective and powerful prayer life*

ISBN: 978-1-60208-445-2

Printed in the USA by
Faith Baptist Church Publications
Fort Pierce, FL 34982
www.fbcpublications.com
772-461-6460

Table Of Contents

Foreword

Men, have you ever desired to have a prayer life like the one stated in James 5:16? It says, "The effectual fervent prayer of a righteous man availeth much." I don't know about you, but I really long to have that kind of prayer life. A prayer life that is more than just rituals and ruts, but one that is truly effective.

Let's face it, prayer is a battle. We will fight distractive thoughts in our prayer time. We also will fight the forces of evil, as well as, the fatigue of our own flesh. How can I get victory in my prayer time? I think there are three keys for every Christian man to obtain victory in prayer. These keys are found in Mark 11:22-26. **"And Jesus answering them saith unto them, Have faith in God. For verily I say unto you, That whosoever shall say unto this mountain, Be thou removed, and be thou cast into the sea; and shall not doubt in his heart, but shall believe that those things which he saith shall come to pass; he shall have whatsoever he saith. Therefore I say unto you, What things soever ye desire, when ye pray, believe that ye receive them, and ye shall have them. And when ye stand praying, forgive, if ye have ought against any: that your Father also which is in heaven may forgive you your trespasses. But if ye do not forgive, neither will your Father which is in heaven forgive your trespasses."**

These keys have nothing to do with the loudness of your voice, the length of your time, or the lingo of your words. Here are the keys to an effective prayer life. First, there is **faith**. When we mention faith, we are not talking about faith in faith. We are talking about faith in God. Our faith rests in His word. It is so important that our faith be anchored to His truth because this is how we come to know

God. Romans 10:17, "Faith cometh by hearing and hearing by the word of God." An effective prayer life is anchored in the precepts, principles, and promises of God. We need to pray according to the scriptures. That is why it is necessary to lift up God's word in prayer. Your prayers should grow as your knowledge of God increases. Have faith in God. The Lord and His word are truth.

The next key is found in the word **believe.** This is where we move from the truth of God's word, to the trust of God's word. I believe what God said. This is not about us getting our will done from earth to heaven, but it is about God's will being done from heaven to earth. When we believe and pray the word of God, we are trusting in the Lord's greatness and His faithfulness. We trust the Lord's greatness in the fact that nothing is too hard for Him and that He is so great that He cannot make a mistake. His "no's" are just as great as His "yes's." I can trust God regardless of the size of my request because He is great. We also trust the Lord's faithfulness when we pray. The Lord is faithful to hear, answer, and help in our request. Whether we feel like our prayer was heard or not, the Lord God of heaven is faithful to hear us period. What a privilege we have been given through prayer. When we trust and rest on the faithfulness and the greatness of God, we have confidence that the outcome will be right.

The final key is found in the word **forgive.** This has to do with our testimony before God. It is imperative that we be right with God and right with our fellow man when we pray. This means that we must give up that grudge or bitterness that has come through the mistreatment of others. Sometimes to receive from God through prayer we must release to God through prayer. Unforgiveness will hold back your fellowship with God. I'm so thankful that we can confess our sins to God and know that He is faithful and just to forgive us our sins and to cleanse us from all unrighteousness. We must be clean before God if we expect to receive from God.

I hope this book will be a guide for your prayer life. I want this book to be a model to help you in prayer, not a book to be just recited in prayer. Praying is a battle. We need some men to step up and fight the good fight of faith in the war room of prayer. Let's be men that would have a prayer life that is effective. May God bless you as you step into the battle of prayer.

Praise and Confessions

Praises of a praying man

1 Thessalonians 5:18 "In everything give thanks: for this is the will of God in Christ Jesus concerning you."

Psalm 95:2a "Let us come before his presence with thanksgiving..."

Psalm 100:4 "Enter into his gates with thanksgiving, and into his courts with praise: be thankful unto him, and bless his name."

Psalm 118:1 "O give thanks unto the LORD; for he is good: because his mercy endureth for ever."

Ephesians 5:20 "Giving thanks always for all things unto God and the Father in the name of our Lord Jesus Christ."

Lord, You have blessed me more than I could ever say. You have provided, forgiven, protected, and extended grace and mercy to me over and over again. You have redeemed me and washed away my sins. You are patient with me and offer forgiveness each and every day. You have answered prayers and I praise You.

Psalm 77:11 "I will remember the works of the LORD: surely I will remember thy wonders of old."

Psalm 105:5 "Remember his marvelous works that he hath done; his wonders, and the judgments of his mouth."

Psalm 143:5 "I remember the days of old; I meditate on all thy works; I muse on the work of thy hands."

Lord, You have done so many wonderful things for me. If I stop and think of all the answers to prayer over the years it will encourage me when I face the yet to be answered prayers of the future. So, today I will take time and remember. Thank You for:

Confessions of a praying man

Psalm 51:1-2 "Have mercy upon me, O God, according to thy loving kindness: according unto the multitude of thy tender mercies blot out my transgressions. Wash me thoroughly from mine iniquity, and cleanse me from my sin."

Proverbs 28:13 "He that covereth his sins shall not prosper: but whoso confesseth and forsaketh them shall have mercy."

Psalm 32:5 "I acknowledged my sin unto thee, and mine iniquity have I not hid. I said, I will confess my transgressions unto the LORD; and thou forgavest the iniquity of my sin. Selah."

1 John 1:8-9 "If we say that we have no sin, we deceive ourselves, and the truth is not in us. If we confess our sins, he is faithful and just to forgive us our sins, and to cleanse us from all unrighteousness."

Lord, I thank You for Your forgiveness. I choose today to acknowledge my sin. Lord, I confess to you my sin of ____________. Open my eyes to it, Lord. May I not be deceived. May I not excuse, rename, or turn a blind eye to my sins. There are sin cycles and habits present in me. I confess them to You. I confess it to You as sin and ask You to cleanse me and to help me to overcome this sin and its pattern in my life.

Specific verses and prayers for my own personal weaknesses:

Prayers of forgiveness

A Praying Man Must Forgive

Lord, Your word tells me that I must forgive those that have done me wrong.

Colossians 3:12-13 "Put on therefore, as the elect of God, holy and beloved, bowels of mercies, kindness, humbleness of mind, meekness, longsuffering; Forbearing one another, and forgiving one another, if any man have a quarrel against any: even as Christ forgave you, so also do ye."

Ephesians 4:30-32 "And grieve not the holy Spirit of God, whereby ye are sealed unto the day of redemption. Let all bitterness, and wrath, and anger, and clamour, and evil speaking, be put away from you, with all malice: And be ye kind one to another, tenderhearted, forgiving one another, even as God for Christ's sake hath forgiven you."

Lord, Your Word is clear. I am commanded to forgive as You have forgiven me. Bitterness is wrong and it will cause my prayer life to be blocked. Choosing to forgive is not about the other person, it is about my fellowship with You being unhindered. My communion with you means more to me than my anger does. I choose to release the anger and receive the blessing of living in complete obedience to You.

Matthew 6:14 "For if ye forgive men their trespasses, your heavenly Father will also forgive you."

Mark 11:26 "But if ye do not forgive, neither will your Father which is in heaven forgive your trespasses."

Lord, these verses are very clear. If I want forgiveness, I have to give it. I cannot freely receive this gift, if I do not give this gift. I must have Your forgiveness. I stand in need of it daily. I will not allow the wrong this person did to me to cause me to do wrong. I will not give them that power over me. To forgive them is not to say that what they did was alright. It wasn't. But I want to be alright and in order to do so, I must forgive and with Your help, I can.

Lord, I have been bitter toward _________________. I confess that bitterness as sin. I do not want to grieve You with this sin and so I decide to release these feelings of anger, hatred, and bitterness. I will forgive as You have forgiven me. You forgive me when I do not deserve it. You forgive me over and over again. You forgive me when I am at my worst. I now turn and offer that same forgiveness to this person. I make this choice now, in this moment, realizing I will have to make it again tomorrow and the next day and the day after that. I will not wait on my feelings. I will make the choice to forgive based on obedience. I choose You, Lord. I submit to You, Lord. I will obey, Lord. I ask You to supernaturally enable me to do what will go against my nature and that is to extend forgiveness. I need Your divine empowerment to do this and that is what I ask for in the name of Jesus.

Write out your own verses and prayer of forgiveness below.

____

____

Head to toe prayers

My Mind

Lord, my mind is such a battlefield. The battle of a victorious Christian life will be won or lost on this particular battlefield. I need to realize the significance of it. I need to know the importance of paying attention to what I think. I need to think about my thinking. Help me to choose to do that today.

1 Chronicles 28:9b "...know thou the God of thy father, and serve him with a perfect heart and a willing mind; for the LORD searcheth all hearts, and understandeth all the imaginations of the thoughts: if thou seek him, he will be found of thee..."

Job 42:2 "I know that thou canst do every thing, and that no thought can be witholden from thee."

Psalm 94:11 "The LORD knoweth the thoughts of man, that they are vanity."

Psalm 139:2, 23 and 24 "Thou knowest my downsitting and mine uprising, thou understandest my thought afar off. Search me, O God, and know my heart: try me, and know my thoughts; And see if there be any wicked way in me, and lead me in the way everlasting."

Lord, You are amazing. You hold the universe in Your hands, yet You know my every thought. You know the good ones, the bad ones, and the ugly ones. There is nothing hidden from you. I praise You today for knowing me inside and out and choosing to love me despite my weaknesses. Help me to choose to love other people in my life despite their weaknesses. Help me to give people room to be weak and to be human. Help me to offer grace.

Philippians 4:8 "Finally, brethren, whatsoever things are true, whatsoever things are honest, whatsoever things are just, whatsoever things are pure, whatsoever things are lovely, whatsoever things are of good report; if there be any virtue, and if there be any praise, think on these things."

Lord, you know what I am struggling with in my mind today. Is it true, honest, just, pure, lovely, of good report? Does it promote virtue or praise? If not, then Lord, I choose to lay it down and think on things that are true, honest, just, pure, lovely, and of good report. That is my choice. I choose virtue and praise in my thoughts today.

Isaiah 26:3 "Thou wilt keep him in perfect peace, whose mind is stayed on thee: because he trusteth in thee."

Philippians 4:7 "And the peace of God, which passeth all understanding, shall keep your hearts and minds through Christ Jesus."

2 Timothy 1:7 "For God hath not given us the spirit of fear; but of power, and of love, and of a sound mind."

Lord, I pray for your perfect peace to keep my mind today. This is a result of trusting in you. When peace flees it is because trust fled first. Today, I choose to trust you instead of dwelling in fear because that spirit doesn't come from you. I will live this day in trust and in peace instead of fear.

Philippians 2:3-5 "Let nothing be done through strife or vainglory; but in lowliness of mind let each esteem other better than themselves. Look not every man on his own things, but every man also on the things of others. Let this mind be in you, which was also in Christ Jesus."

Romans 12:3 "For I say, through the grace given unto me, to every man that is among you, not to think of himself more highly than he ought to think; but to think soberly, according as God hath dealt to every man the measure of faith."

Lord, help me to realize that selfish thoughts lead to selfish and hurtful actions. The world does not revolve around me. If I am constantly aggravated or easily angered, it is because I am thinking pridefully and selfishly. I lay down those selfish thoughts and that self-centered way of thinking today. I choose to put the needs of others above my own today. This is the choice I choose to make today.

1 Peter 1:13 "Wherefore gird up the loins of your mind..."

2 Corinthians 10:5 "Casting down imaginations, and every high thing that exalteth itself against the knowledge of God, and bringing into captivity every thought to the obedience of Christ."

1 Corinthians 10:12 "Wherefore let him that thinketh he standeth take heed lest he fall."

Lord, the strongholds in my mind are very real. Today, I confess _______________. Those kinds of thoughts are wrong. They are sin. I ask for your supernatural enabling and divine empowering to overcome them in the name of Jesus.

Psalm 119:59 "I thought on my ways, and turned my feet unto thy testimonies."

Lord, if I do not think about my thinking and my sin cycles and patterns in my life, I will just repeat them over and over. I choose to think on my ways today and to deliberately turn to YOUR ways. Today, help me to make one different choice so that I will stop doing what I have always done. Open my eyes to the satanic lies I have listened to for a very long time and help me to turn toward You and go down a different path today.

Proverbs 24:9a "The thought of foolishness is sin..."

Lord, to even think sinful thoughts is sin. For these sinful thoughts lead to sinful actions. May I stop it right here. If I do not want to act wrong, then I cannot think wrong. Help me to stop the stinking thinking. Help me to see it, recognize it, and confess it right away. May my mind be holy. May it not be a breeding ground for sin.

Proverbs 12:5 "The thoughts of the righteous are right: but the counsels of the wicked are deceit."

Proverbs 16:3 "Commit thy works unto the LORD, and thy thoughts shall be established."

Lord, help me to be righteous so that my thoughts are righteous. Today, I commit my works unto You. Please establish my thoughts, I pray.

Write out your own verses, requests, and prayers concerning your mind.

My Eyes

Lord, what I look at matters to You. What I see makes a difference in what I think and in what I feel. The images the world places before me are deliberate and not random. They are part of a master plan the enemy has. May I realize this and be just as deliberate in how I pray over what my eyes behold. Help me to guard what I set before my eyes, personally as this is a weakness in my life.

Psalm 33:18 and 19 "Behold the eyè of the LORD is upon them that fear him, upon them that hope in his mercy; To deliver their soul from death, and to keep them alive in famine."

Psalm 116:8 "For thou hast delivered my soul from death, mine eyes from tears, and my feet from falling."

Proverbs 15:3 "The eyes of the LORD are in every place, beholding the evil and the good."

Lord, thank You that You see me. You know right where I am and will never forsake me. You know exactly what I am facing and what is going on in my life. You see when wrongs are done to me and when I do wrong. Help me to keep that in mind as I go about my day.

Psalm 119:18 "Open thou mine eyes, that I may behold wondrous things out of thy law."

Psalm 19:8 "The statutes of the LORD are right, rejoicing the heart: the commandment of the LORD is pure, enlightening the eyes."

Lord, help me to see what You are trying to say to me through Your Word. Open my eyes to Your truths and speak to my heart concerning them.

Psalm 5:3 "My voice shalt thou hear in the morning, O LORD; in the morning will I direct my prayer unto thee and will look up."

Psalm 121:1 and 2 "I will lift up mine eyes unto the hills, from whence cometh my help. My help cometh from the LORD, which made heaven and earth."

Lord, I choose to look to You for my help and not to another person, myself, or trying to logically figure out the next step. I will not force doors to open or manipulate to bring about what I want to happen. I will look only to You and realize You are my help and I will rest in knowing You are completely in control. Help me not to try to manipulate the situation or other people in my life in order to get the upper hand. I will trust You instead.

Psalm 101:3 "I will set no wicked thing before mine eyes: I hate the work of them that turn aside; it shall not cleave to me."

2 Corinthians 10:7 "Do ye look on things after the outward appearance? If any man trust to himself that he is Christ's, let him of himself think this again, that, he is Christ's, even so are we Christ's."

1 John 2:15-17 "Love not the world, neither the things that are in the world. If any man love the world, the love of the Father is not in him. For all that is in the world, the lust of the flesh, and the lust of the eyes, and the pride of life, is

not of the Father, but is of the world. And the world passeth away, and the lust thereof but he that doeth the will of God abideth for ever."

Lord, guard my eyes today. May I set nothing wicked in front of them on purpose, and may nothing wicked be put in front of them by accident. I pray for my perceptions today, the eyes of my mind and emotions. Help me to perceive and view things as they actually are and not what I assume them to be. May I not have distorted lenses over my eyes coloring things as I view life through lenses of selfishness and self-centeredness, past pain and disappointment, regret or anger. May I perceive You as You really are so that I can perceive everything else appropriately. Help me to see things from the eyes of others and how they perceive them. May I understand and respect their point of view today and every day.

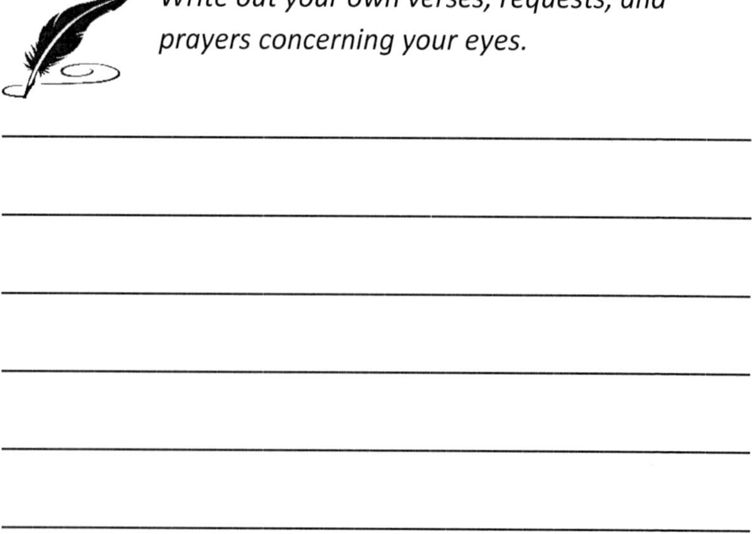

Write out your own verses, requests, and prayers concerning your eyes.

My Ears

Lord, help me to be a good listener. So many times, I am formulating my own response, not paying attention, tempted to interrupt, or am simply not patient enough to truly listen to others. I pray over my ears that I would become a good listener.

Nehemiah 1:6a "Let thine ear now be attentive, and thine eyes open, that thou mayest hear the prayer of thy servant, which I pray before thee now, day and night…"

Psalm 10:17 "LORD, thou hast heard the desire of the humble: thou wilt prepare their heart, thou wilt cause thine ear to hear."

Psalm 6:9 "The LORD hath heard my supplication; the LORD will receive my prayer."

Psalm 116:1 "I LOVE the LORD, because he hath heard my voice and my supplications."

Isaiah 59:1 "BEHOLD the LORD'S hand is not shortened, that it cannot save; neither his ear heavy, that it cannot hear."

Lord, thank You that You hear my cry. Thank You that You are in tune with Your children and hear not only our words but our hearts as well.

Psalm 85:8 "I will hear what God the LORD will speak: for he will speak peace unto his people, and to his saints: but let them not turn again to folly."

Proverbs 15:31 and 32 "The ear that heareth the reproof of life abideth among the wise. He that refuseth instruction despiseth his own soul: but he that heareth reproof getteth understanding."

Lord, may I be teachable. May my ears be attentive and my spirit humble so I can learn from You. May I be discerning and wise in who I listen to. Surround me with wise and godly counsel I pray.

Proverbs 18:15b "...the ear of the wise seeketh knowledge."

Proverbs 22:17 "Bow down thine ear, and hear the words of the wise, and apply thine heart unto my knowledge."

Isaiah 50:4 "The Lord GOD hath given me the tongue of the learned, that I should know how to speak a word in season to him that is weary: he wakeneth morning by morning, he wakeneth mine ear to hear as the learned."

Jeremiah 9:20a "Yet hear the word of the LORD, . . ."

John 8:47a "He that is of God heareth God's words..."

James 1:19 "Wherefore, my beloved brethren, let every man be swift to hear, slow to speak, slow to wrath."

Romans 10:17 "So then faith cometh by hearing, and hearing by the word of God."

Lord, You gave me TWO ears and only ONE mouth. Help me to listen twice as much as I speak. Help me to listen to YOU and to Your Word. Help me to heed, to hearken, and to learn. May I turn down the noise of this world so that I can hear Your still small voice. Help me to turn down the noise of my selfish desires, wayward emotions and thoughts, and the lies of Satan. May I walk away from critical conversations and not give them a listening ear. Then and only then, will I hear from You.

Write out your own verses, requests, and prayers concerning your ears.

My Mouth

Lord, help me to be very aware of the dangers of my tongue. Every word I say today I will have to answer for. May that reality be ever before me. May I choose my words wisely and carefully all day long.

James 3:5 and 6 "Even so the tongue is a little member, and boasteth great things, Behold, how great a matter a little fire kindleth! And the tongue is a fire, a world of iniquity: so is the tongue among our members, that it defileth the whole body, and setteth on fire the course of nature; and it is set on fire of hell."

Matthew 12:36 "But I say unto you, That every idle word that men shall speak, they shall give account thereof in the day of judgment."

Proverbs 18:21a "Death and life are in the power of the tongue..."

Lord, help me not to have a doubleminded tongue saying one thing to someone's face and another behind their back.

James 3:8-11 "But the tongue can no man tame: it is an unruly evil full of deadly poison. Therewith bless we God, even the father; and therewith curse we men, which are made after the similitude of God. Out of the same mouth proceedeth blessing and cursing. My brethren, these things ought not so to be. Doth a fountain send forth at the same place sweet water and bitter?"

Ezekiel 33:31 "And they come unto thee as the people cometh, and they sit before thee as my people, and they

hear thy words, but they will not do them: for with their mouth they shew much love, but their heart goeth after their covetousness."

James 1:26 "If any man among you seem to be religious, and bridleth not his tongue, but deceiveth his own heart, this man's religion is vain."

Matthew 12:34 "O generation of vipers, how can ye, being evil, speak good things? For out of the abundance of the heart the mouth speaketh."

Lord, help me to be determined to keep my tongue under YOUR control.

Psalm 141:3 "Set a watch, O LORD, before my mouth, keep the door of my lips."

Philippians 2:14 "Do all things without murmurings and disputings."

Psalm 39:1 "I SAID, I will take heed to my ways, that I sin not with my tongue: I will keep my mouth with a bridle, while the wicked is before me."

Psalm 34:13 "Keep thy tongue from evil, and thy lips from speaking guile."

Psalm 17:3b "...I am purposed that my mouth shall not transgress."

Ephesians 4:29 "Let no corrupt communication proceed out of your mouth, but that which is good to the use of edifying, that it may minister grace unto the hearers."

Proverbs 29:11 "A fool uttereth all his mind: but a wise man keepeth it in till afterwards.

Proverbs 15:4 "A wholesome tongue is a tree of life: but perverseness therein is a breach in the spirit."

Proverbs 18:13 "He that answereth a matter before he heareth it, it is folly and shame unto him."

Proverbs 21:23 "Whoso keepeth his mouth and his tongue keepeth his soul from troubles."

Lord, fill my mouth with good things and give me the right words to say at the right times. Help me to encourage and minister grace to everyone around me. When I have to bring up a tough subject, help me to have wisdom concerning the right time to bring it up. Help me to be careful to maintain the right spirit and motivation before I bring it up and while it is being discussed. May I always have the wisdom to cover the words that I speak in prayer.

Proverbs 15:23 "A man hath joy by the answer of his mouth: and a word spoken in due season, how good is it."

Luke 21:15 "For I will give you a mouth and wisdom, which all your adversaries shall not be able to gainsay nor resist."

Isaiah 50:4a "The Lord GOD hath given me the tongue of the learned, that I should know how to speak a word in season to him that is weary..."

Ephesians 4:25 "Wherefore putting away lying, speak every man truth with his neighbour: for we are members one of another."

Ephesians 4:15 "But speaking the truth in love, may grow up into him in all things, which is the head, even Christ."

Colossians 4:6 "Let your speech be always with grace, seasoned with salt, that ye may know how ye ought to answer every man."

Titus 2:8 "Sound speech, that cannot be condemned; that he that is of the contrary part may be ashamed, having no evil thing to say of you."

Lord, may every word today make you proud. May I please you and edify others with my speech. They are my choice. May I think before I speak and choose each word wisely. My tongue can bring death or life. Today, I choose life.

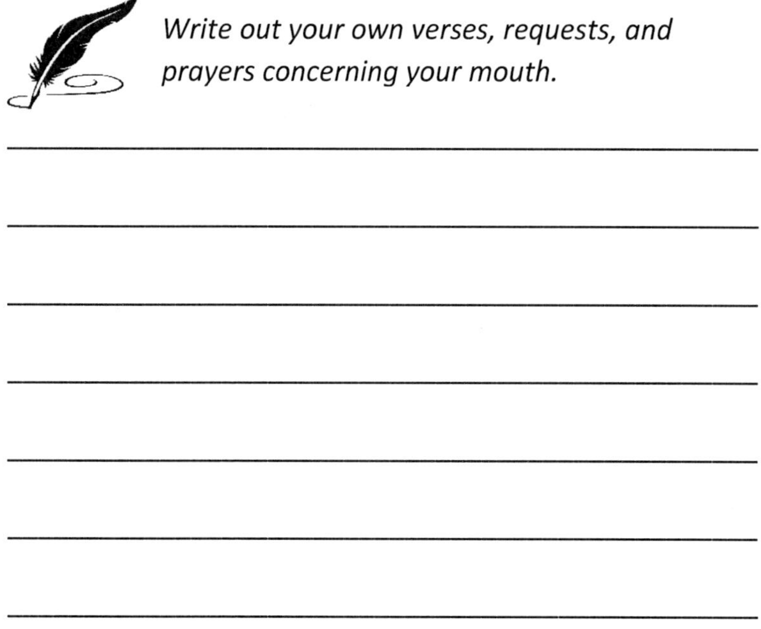

Write out your own verses, requests, and prayers concerning your mouth.

My Heart

Lord, my thoughts and my emotions go hand in hand. Every thought gives birth to an emotion. What I do with that emotion then gives birth to my actions. Thought – emotion – action. If I coddle wicked and sinful emotions, then my actions will also be wicked and sinful. It isn't wrong to have emotions such as sadness, grief, anger, and disappointment. It is what I choose to do with those emotions that turn to sin. If I nurse them, rehearse them, or disperse them I have then chosen to allow them to turn into sin. I can be angry and sin not. I can be sad and sin not. I can be disappointed and sin not. Help me, Lord, to see that line in the sand of my heart and not cross it. I can have these emotions without them having me. I choose to put You in the driver's seat of my heart and my emotions. . .

Proverbs 23:7a "For as he thinketh in his heart, so is he..."

Luke 6:45b "...for of the abundance of the heart his mouth speaketh."

Mark 7:21-23 "For from within, out of the heart of men, proceed evil thoughts, adulteries, fornications, murders, thefts, coveteousness, wickedness, deceit, lasciviousness, an evil eye, blasphemy, pride, foolisness: All these evil things come from within, and defile the man.

Acts 8:22 "Repent therefore of this thy wickedness, and pray God, if perhaps the thought of thine heart may be forgiven thee."

Lord, there is nothing more deceitful than that thing that beats in my chest. I will be deceived and blind to the sin in it unless You open my eyes and show me. I can go through my life totally deceived and doomed to stay stuck in my sin, or I can choose to invite You to search me. I choose to open my eyes to the truth of my heart today.

Jeremiah 17:9 "The heart is deceitful above all things, and desperately wicked: who can know it?"

Psalm 139:23 "Search me, O God, and know my heart: try me, and know my thoughts: And see if there be any wicked way in me, and lead me in the way everlasting."

Acts 11:23b "...that with purpose of heart they would cleave unto the Lord."

Lord, help me to realize that the troubles I go through are sometimes from Your hand. They are for a purpose and that purpose is to soften my heart. They can drive me to You, if I will let them. Today, I give You my heart. Teach and instruct me and help me to have a soft heart. Uncover the true motives of my heart, I ask and pray.

Job 23:16 "For God maketh my heart soft and the Almighty troubleth me."

Ezekiel 11:19 "And I will give them one heart, and I will put a new spirit within you; and I will take the stony heart out of their flesh, and will give them an heart of flesh."

Hebrews 4:12 "For the word of God is quick, and powerful, and sharper than any twoedged sword, piercing even to the dividing asunder of soul and spirit, and of the joints

and marrow, and is a discerner of the thoughts and intents of the heart."

Hebrews 10:22 "Let us draw near with a true heart in full assurance of faith, having our hearts sprinkled from an evil conscience, and our bodies washed with pure water."

James 4:8 "Draw nigh unto God, and he will draw nigh to you. Cleanse your hands ye sinners; and purify your hearts, ye double minded."

Lord, may I hold nothing back from You. May I serve You with all my heart. I want You to be my treasure.

1 Samuel 12:24 "Only fear the LORD, and serve him in truth with all your heart: for consider how great things he hath done for you."

Luke 10:27 "And he answering said, Thou shalt love the Lord thy God with all thy heart, and with all thy soul, and with all thy strength, and with all thy mind; and thy neighbor as thyself.

Luke 12:34 "For where your treasure is, there will your heart be also."

Ephesians 6:6b "...doing the will of God from the heart."

Lord, I need and want a discerning heart. Help me to discern between good and bad and between right and wrong. Satan will try to disguise wrong. He will dress it up as something good at first. Help me to have the God-given discernment to see through that disguise right from the start. Lord, I cannot do that apart from a divine discernment that can only come from You.

1 Kings 3:9a "Give therefore thy servant an understanding heart to judge thy people, that I may discern between good and bad..."

Lord, my heart can be fearful or confident. I want a confident heart today. I choose You over fear. My heart can trust in You and be helped, or I can trust in myself and be a spiritual wreck. If I want a rejoicing heart, I must choose to trust in You. My help, my grounding, my stable heart will come from Your Word. Help me to have a sound established heart in You and one that sings.

Psalm 27:3 "Though an host should encamp against me, my heart shall not fear: though war should rise against me, in this will I be confident."

John 14:27 "Peace I leave with you, my peace I give unto you: not as the world giveth, give I unto you. Let not your heart be troubled, neither let it be afraid."

Philippians 4:7 "And the peace of God, which passeth all understanding shall keep your hearts and minds through Christ Jesus."

Psalm 28:7 "The LORD is my strength and my shield; my heart trusted in him, and I am helped: therefore my heart greatly rejoiceth; and with my song will I praise him."

Ephesians 5:19b "...singing and making melody in your heart to the Lord."

Psalm 119:80 "Let my heart be sound in thy statutes; that I be not ashamed."

Lord, today I am determined to keep my heart and to keep it diligently. All the issues I have can be traced back to my heart. If I want my issues fixed, I have to fix my heart. I can't do it but You can. Here's my heart, Lord. Fix it.

Proverb 4:23 "Keep thy heart with all diligence; for out of it are the issues of life."

Write out your own verses, requests, and prayers concerning your heart and emotions.

____

____

____

____

____

____

____

____

____

____

____

____

My Shoulders

Lord, help me to realize that my shoulders are not built to carry my burdens. Only Your shoulders can carry them. Mine are not strong enough. Help me to realize that I do not have to carry this load. I can cast it upon You, and walk away free of it. I do not have to fix these problems or situations. As your child, I can rest and be sure that You have this and You make no mistakes. Thank You for being able and in control of it all.

Psalm 55:22 "Cast thy burden upon the LORD, and he shall sustain thee: he shall never suffer the righteous to be moved."

Philippians 4:6 "Be careful for nothing but in every thing by prayer and supplication with thanksgiving let your requests be made known unto God.

1 Peter 5:7 "Casting all your care upon him: for he careth for you."

Acts 15:28 "For it seemed good to the Holy Ghost, and to us, to lay upon you no greater burden than these necessary things."

Matthew 11:28 "Come unto me, all ye that labour and are heavy laden, and I will give you rest."

Lord, help me come along side someone this week who is under a load. Help me to show them love, concern, and authenticity. Help me to ask questions and to really listen. Help me to think of someone who needs a shoulder to lean on and to offer it. Help me to get out of my world, my busyness, and my problems and to help another one carry their burden to You. Open my eyes, Lord. And then may I be obedient to do what You show me to do.

1 Corinthians 12:25 "That there should be no schism in the body; but that the members should have the same care one for another."

Galatians 6:2 "Bear ye one another's burdens, and so fulfil the law of Christ."

Write out your own verses, requests, and prayers concerning your shoulders and your burdens.

My Waist and My Knees

Lord, may I bow and surrender to Your will today. Just as You did in the garden, Jesus, so I must surrender my wants and my desires to Your plan and Your design for my life. May I fully realize and believe that Your will for me is best and that You will not withhold any good thing from me. Your no's are just as inspired as Your yes's, Lord. Help me to live like I really believe that. Help me to trust You to be who You say You are. Help me to live out the truth that You are for me and that You make no mistake.

Lord, You will work out everything FOR me.

Romans 8:28 "And we know that all things work together for good to them that love God, to them who are the called according to his purpose."

Lord, You will work everything out AROUND me.

Ephesians 1:11 "In whom also we have obtained an inheritance, being predestinated according to the purpose of him who worketh all things after the counsel of his own will."

Lord, You will work out everything IN me.

Philippians 2:13 "For it is God which worketh in you both to will and to do of his good pleasure."

Lord, I really want things to work out a certain way but it isn't about me and my desires and wishes. I lay this situation down and I lay down my will too. I pray, not my will but thine be done, Lord.

Matthew 26:39-42 "And he went a little farther and fell on his face, and prayed saying, O my Father, if it be possible, let this cup pass from me nevertheless not as I will, but as thou wilt...He went away again the second time, and prayed saying O my Father, if this cup may not pass away from me, except I drink it, thy will be done."

Lord, I choose to submit to You today. I submit my plans, my will, and my desires to You. I choose to resist the temptation to control and get my hands on this situation as well as all the details surrounding it.

James 4:7 "Submit yourselves therefore to God. Resist the devil, and he will flee from you."

Lord, I choose to submit to the earthly authorities You have placed over me. You have set up life to be checks and balances. I place myself willingly under these authorities knowing they are fallible and human. They are not perfect, but neither am I. I will choose to submit because that is my responsibility. That is all I will answer for. They will answer for their actions. As for me, I will be obedient.

1 Peter 2:13-19 "Submit yourselves to every ordinance of man for the Lord's sake: whether it be to the king, as supreme; Or unto governors, as unto them that are sent by him for the punishment of evildoers, and for the praise of them that do well. For so is the will of God, that with well doing ye may put to silence the ignorance of foolish men...Honor all men, Love the brotherhood. Fear God. Honour the king. Servants, be subject to your masters with all fear; not only to the good and gentle, but also to

the forward. For this is thankworthy if a man for conscience toward God endure grief, suffering wrongfully.

Ephesians 5:21 "Submitting yourselves one to another in the fear of God."

Write out your own verses, requests, and prayers concerning your waist, knees, bowing, and surrendering.

My Hands and My Feet

Lord, my hands and my feet are to be holy and to be busy doing holy and righteous things. My steps are to be honest and quick to bring good news to others. May my feet and hands be busy bringing the truth of the gospel to others this week. My hands and feet were created to spread peace, truth, knowledge of You, and to help others. My hands and feet are not to be lazy, sinful, or discouraging in any way. May I be able to look back at my day today and see where I have done good deeds and where I have made a difference with my hands and my feet. May my hands serve others this week and may I find ways to be a blessing to those who are around me.

1 Thessalonians 4:11,12 "And that ye study to be quiet, and to do your own business, and to work with your own hands, as we commanded you; That ye may walk honestly toward them that are without, and that ye may have lack of nothing."

Zephaniah 3:16b "Let not thine hands be slack."

1 Timothy 2:8 "I will therefore that men pray every where, lifting up holy hands, without wrath and doubting."

James 4:8 "Draw nigh to God, and he will draw nigh to you. Cleanse your hands, ye sinners; and purify your hearts, ye double minded."

Romans 10:15b "...How beautiful are the feet of them that preach the gospel of peace and bring glad tidings of good things!"

Isaiah 52:7 "How beautiful upon the mountains are the feet of him that bringeth good tidings, that publisheth peace; that bringeth good tidings of good, that publisheth salvation; that saith unto Zion, Thy God reigneth!"

1 John 3:18 "My little children, let us not love in word, neither in tongue; but in deed and in truth."

Isaiah 56:2 "Blessed is the man that...keepeth his hand from doing any evil."

Psalm 24:3-5 "Who shall ascend into the hill of the LORD? or who shall stand in his holy place? He that hath clean hands, and a pure heart; who hath not lifted up his soul unto vanity, nor sworn deceitfully. He shall receive the blessing from the LORD and righteousness from the God of his salvation."

Lord, picking a fight with another person is not a place I should go. If I look for reasons to get mad, I will find them. If I pick on the weaknesses of others, that isn't peace.

Luke 1:79b "...to guide our feet into the way of peace."

Lord, I do not want to step outside of your will. I want to make the right choices and do the right things. Guide my steps, Lord, so that I do not fall – fall into sin, fall into wrong and destructive habits, fall into dangerous relationships, fall into selfishness, or fall into the wrong decisions. Lead me and may I willingly follow the steps You lay before me.

Psalm 116:8 "For thou hast delivered my soul from death, mine eyes from tears, and my feet from falling."

Psalm 18:36 "For thou hast enlarged my steps under me, that my feet did not slip."

Psalm 119:105 "Thy word is a lamp unto my feet, and a light unto my path."

Lord, I have a work to do in my home, marriage, my job, and my ministries. Establish the work of my hands. May I build up and never tear down. Strengthen my hands in this work because I will get tired in it. When I do, help me, strengthen me, and fill me with resolve to do the right thing and not give into the flesh. May my hands build up and encourage all those around me I pray.

Psalm 90:17 "And let the beauty of the LORD our God be upon us: and establish thou the work of our hands upon us; yea, the work of our hands establish thou it."

Nehemiah 2:18 "Then I told them of the hand of my God which was good upon me; as also the king's words that he had spoken unto me. And they said, Let us rise up and build. So they strengthened their hands for this good work."

Write out your own verses, requests, and prayers concerning your hands, feet, and works.

____

____

____

____

Declarations

Declarations of who I am in Christ

Lord, my heart will lie to me. There are some facts that are true whether I feel them or not and these are found in Your word. There will be days when I doubt everything I believe to be true. There will be moments that Satan will paint You in a very negative light, if I let him. I choose not to. Help me to be determined not to doubt in the dark what You have assured me of in the light. Sometimes my prayer time will need to be declarations of what I KNOW to be true not what I FEEL to be true. Today and every day I choose to believe FACT over FEELINGS. I choose to believe even when it is hard, when it hurts, and when I do not understand and nothing in my life makes sense anymore.

Luke 1:1 "Forasmuch as many have taken in hand to set forth in order a declaration of those things which are most surely believed among us."

Lord, today I set forth some declarations about me that I most surely believe. I will no longer allow Satan to put a question mark where You have placed a period.

I am Redeemed.

Psalm 31:5 "Into thine hand I commit my spirit: thou has redeemed me, O LORD God of truth."

Psalm 106:10 "And he saved them from the hand of him that hated them, and redeemed them from the hand of the enemy."

Isaiah 43:1 "But now thus saith the LORD that created thee, O Jacob, and he that formed thee, O Israel, Fear not: for I have redeemed thee, I have called thee by thy name, thou art mine."

I am set free.

Romans 6:18 "Being then made free from sin, ye became the servants of righteousness."

Romans 6:22 "But now being made free from sin, and become servants to God, ye have your fruit unto holiness, and the end everlasting life."

Romans 8:2 "For the law of the Spirit of life in Christ Jesus hath made me free from the law of sin and death."

Galatians 5:1 "Stand fast therefore in the liberty wherewith Christ hath made us free, and be not entangled again with the yoke of bondage."

I am forgiven.

Ephesians 1:7 "In whom we have redemption through his blood, the forgiveness of sins, according to the riches of his grace."

Hebrews 8:12 "For I will be merciful to their unrighteousness, and their sins and their iniquities will I remember no more."

Isaiah 43:25 "I, even I, am he that blotteth out thy transgressions for mine own sake, and will not remember thy sins."

Psalm 103:12 "As far as the east is from the west, so far hath he removed our transgressions from us."

Psalm 130:3-4a "If thou, LORD, shouldest mark iniquities, O Lord, who shall stand: But there is forgiveness with thee…"

I am clean.

John 15:3 "Now ye are clean through the word which I have spoken unto you."

I am without blame.

Ephesians 1:4 "According as he hath chosen us in him before the foundation of the world, that we should be holy and without blame before him in love."

1 Thessalonians 5:23 "And the very God of peace sanctify you wholly; and I pray God your whole spirit and soul and body be preserved blameless unto the coming of our Lord Jesus Christ."

I can through Christ.

Philippians 4:13 "I can do all things through Christ which strengtheneth me."

2 Peter 1:3 "According as his divine power hath given unto us all things that pertain unto life and godliness, through the knowledge of him that hath called us to glory and virtue: Whereby are given unto us exceeding great and precious promises: that by these ye might be partakers of the divine nature, having escaped the corruption that is in the world through lust."

2 Corinthians 9:8 "And God is able to make all grace abound toward you; that ye, always having all sufficiency in all things, may abound to every good work."

I am safe.

Psalm 9:9 "The LORD also will be a refuge for the oppressed, a refuge in times of trouble."

Psalm 59:16 "But I will sing of thy power, yea, I will sing aloud of thy mercy in the morning: for thou hast been my defence and refuge in the day of my trouble."

Psalm 62:8 "Trust in him at all times; ye people, pour out your heart before him: God is a refuge for us. Selah."

1 John 5:18 "There is no fear in love; but perfect love casteth out fear: because fear hath torment. He that feareth is not made perfect in love."

I am loved.

1 John 4:19 "We love him, because he first loved us."

1 John 4:10 "Herein is love, not that we loved God, but that he loved us, and sent his Son to be the propitiation for our sins."

1 John 4:16 "And we have known and believed the love that God hath to us. God is love; and he that dwelleth in love dwelleth in God, and God in him."

1 John 3:1 "Behold, what manner of love the Father hath bestowed upon us, that we should be called the sons of God: therefore the world knoweth us not, because it knew him not."

Galatians 2:20 "I am crucified with Christ: nevertheless I live; yet not I, but Christ liveth in me: and the life that I now live in the flesh I live by the faith of the Son of God, who loved me, and gave himself for me."

Romans 8:38-39 "For I am persuaded, that neither death, nor life, nor angels, nor principalities, nor powers, nor things present, nor things to come, Nor height, nor depth, nor any other creature shall be able to separate us from the love of God, which is in Christ Jesus our Lord"

I am complete.

Colossians 2:10 "And ye are complete in him, which is the head of all principality and power."

Colossians 4:12b "...that ye may stand perfect and complete in all the will of God."

I am strong in Christ.

Philippians 4:13 "I can do all things through Christ which strengtheneth me."

Colossians 1:11a "Strengthened with all might, according to his glorious power..."

Psalm 68:28 "Thy God hath commanded thy strength: strengthen, O God, that which thou hast wrought for us."

Psalm 119:28 "My soul melteth for heaviness: strengthen thou me according unto thy word."

I am God's temple.

1 Corinthians 3:16 "Know ye not that ye are the temple of God, and that the Spirit of God dwelleth in you?"

1 Corinthians 6:19-20 "What? Know ye not that your body is the temple of the Holy Ghost which is in you, which ye have of God, and ye are not your own? For ye are bought with a price: therefore glorify God in your body, and in your spirit, which are God's."

I am worth much.

Psalm 139:14-16 "I will praise thee; for I am fearfully and wonderfully made: marvelous are thy works; and that my soul knoweth right well. My substance was not hid from thee, when I was made in secret, and curiously wrought in the lowest parts of the earth. Thine eyes did see my substance, yet being unperfect; and in thy book all my member were written, which in continuance were fashioned, when as yet there was none of them. How precious also are thy thoughts unto me, O God! how great is the sum of them! If I should count them, they are more in number than the sand; when I awake, I am still with thee."

I am more than a conqueror.

Romans 8:37 "Nay in all these things we are more than conquerors through him that loved us."

I am equipped to change and to live holy.

1 Peter 1:3-4 "According as his divine power hath given unto us all things that pertain unto life and godliness, through the knowledge of him that hath called us to glory and virtue:

Whereby are given unto us exceeding great and precious promises: that by these ye might be partakers of the divine nature, having escaped the corruption that is in the world through lust."

Ephesians 1:3-4 "Blessed be the God and Father of our Lord Jesus Christ, who hath blessed us with all spiritual blessings in heavenly places in Christ: According as he hath chosen us in him before the foundation of the world, that we should be holy and without blame before him in love."

I am royalty. I am a son of God.

John 1:12 "But as many as received him, to them gave he power to become the sons of God, even to them that believe on his name."

Ephesians 2:4-7 "But God, who is rich in mercy, for his great love wherewith he loved us, Even when we were dead in sins, hath quickened us together with Christ, (by grace ye are saved;) And hath raised us up together, and made us sit together in heavenly places in Christ Jesus: That in the ages to come he might shew the exceeding riches of his grace in his kindness toward us through Christ Jesus."

I am blessed.

Psalm 2:12b "...Blessed are all they that put their trust in him."

Psalm 32:1 "Blessed is he whose transgression is forgiven whose sin is covered."

Psalm 34:8 "O taste and see that the LORD is good: blessed is the man that trusteth in him."

Psalm 84:4 "Blessed are they that dwell in thy house: They will be still praising thee. Selah."

Proverbs 28:20a "A faithful man shall abound with blessings..."

Ephesians 1:3 "Blessed be the God and Father of our Lord Jesus Christ, who hath blessed us with all spiritual blessings in heavenly places in Christ."

Psalm 68:19 "Blessed be the Lord, who daily loadeth us with benefits, even the God of our salvation. Selah."

I am accepted.

Ephesians 1:6 "To the praise of the glory of his grace, wherein he hath made us accepted in the beloved."

Write out your own declarations and verses that prove them.

____

____

____

____

____

____

____

Declarations about God - His Identity and His Ability

Luke 1:1 "Forasmuch as many have taken in hand to set forth in order a declaration of those things which are most surely believed among us."

Lord, once again, my heart will lie to me about You when times get hard and trials come. Satan will lie about who You really are. He will paint You as mean, unloving, unkind, weak, and uninvolved. These are lies and I will not believe them when I hear them hissed in my ear. I choose to declare the truth from Your word. I choose to believe what You say about You. I will go to You and trust FACT over FEELING.

You always have been and You always will be. Your name "I AM" shows us this.

Colossians 1:17 "And he is before all things, and by him all things consist."

You know and understand everything.

Psalm 147:5 "Great is our LORD, and of great power: his understanding is infinite.

You never change.

Malachi 3:6a "For I am the LORD, I change not..."

Hebrews 13:8 "Jesus Christ the same yesterday, and to day, and for ever."

You are all powerful.

Psalm 24:8 "Who is this King of glory? The LORD strong and mighty, the LORD mighty in battle."

Genesis 18:14 "Is any thing too hard for the LORD?"

Jeremiah 32:17 "Ah Lord GOD! behold, thou hast made the heaven and the earth by thy great power and stretched out arm, and there is nothing too hard for thee."

Luke 1:37 "For with God nothing shall be impossible."

You know all.

Isaiah 46:9-10 "Remember the former things of old; for I am God, there is none else; I am God, and there is none like me, Declaring the end from the beginning, and from the ancient times the things that are not yet done, saying, My counsel shall stand, and I will do all my pleasure."

You are everywhere.

Psalm 139:7-10 "Whither shall I go from thy spirit? Or whither shall I flee from thy presence? If I ascend up into heaven thou art there: if I make my bed in hell, behold, thou art there. If I take the wings of the morning, and dwell in the uttermost parts of the sea: even there shall thy hand lead me, and thy right hand shall hold me."

You are faithful.

Deuteronomy 7:9 "Know therefore that the LORD thy God, he is God, the faithful God, which keepeth covenant and mercy with them that love him and keep his commandments to a thousand generations."

2 Timothy 2:13 "If we believe not, yet he abideth faithful: he cannot deny himself."

You are good.

Psalm 34:8 "O taste and see that the LORD is good: blessed is the man that trusteth in him."

Psalm 145:9 "The LORD is good to all: and his tender mercies are over all his works."

You are just.

Deuteronomy 32:4 "He is the Rock, his work is perfect: for all his ways are judgment: a God of truth and without iniquity, just and right is he."

You give grace and mercy.

Romans 9:15-16 "For he saith to Moses, I will have mercy on whom I will have mercy, and I will have compassion on whom I will have compassion. So then it is not of him that willeth, nor of him that runneth, but of God that sheweth mercy."

Psalm 145:8 "The LORD is gracious, and full of compassion; slow to anger, and of great mercy."

You are love and You love me.

1 John 4:8-10 "He that loveth not knoweth not God; for God is love. In this was manifested the love of God toward us, because that God sent his only begotten Son into the world, that we might live through him. Herein is love, not that we loved God, but that he loved us and sent his Son to be the propitiation for our sins."

You are holy.

Revelation 4:8b "Holy, holy, holy, Lord God almighty, which was, and is, and is to come."

You are worthy.

Revelation 4:11 "Thou art worthy, O Lord, to receive glory and honour and power: for thou hast created all things, and for thy pleasure thy are and were created."

Revelation 5:12 "Saying with a loud voice, Worthy is the Lamb that was slain to receive power, and riches, and wisdom, and strength, and honour, and glory, and blessing."

Your timing is right.

Ecclesiastes 3:11 "He hath made every thing beautiful in his time: also he hath set the world in their heart, so that no man can find out the work that God maketh from the beginning to the end."

You make no mistake.

2 Samuel 22:31 "As for God, his way is perfect; the word of the LORD is tried: he is a buckler to all them that trust in him."

Write out your own declarations about God and the verses that prove them. You may also want to do a study and write out the names of God and call out specific names in prayers.

____

Marriage Prayers

Head to Toe Prayers for a Husband and Wife

Lord, I pray over our minds today. May we think on things that are true, honest, just, and pure. May we think on lovely things that are of good report. May we have virtuous thoughts that are filled with praise today. Help us today not to rehearse the wrong doings and shortcomings of each other. Please help us to extend grace and to live with one another, wisely. May we choose today to love and to live out our love for each other. May we not allow selfishness to rule our thoughts today.

Lord, I pray over our eyes today. May we view things correctly and not through distorted lenses of hurt, selfishness, and pride. May we not look for flaws in each other. May we choose to focus on the good in each other and be thankful.

Lord, I now pray over our ears. You gave us two of them and only one mouth each. This means we need to listen more and talk less. Help us to be perceptive to the needs of each other and to truly listen. May we be swift to hear and slow to speak.

Lord, I pray over our mouths. Set a watch over our mouths and help us to speak only after we think first. May we not say anything out of anger, impatience, pride, or selfishness today. May our words minister grace to everyone that hears them, but especially to each other. Help us to encourage one another today and to be a blessing. May we understand how to communicate with each other wisely.

Lord, I pray over our hearts today. They are deceitful above all things and desperately wicked. I ask You to search them today and reveal the wickedness that is within. Reveal truth to us and open our eyes to it. May we deliberately choose to lay down our rights and pick up our responsibilities. May we choose to lay aside selfishness and our self-centered tendencies. May we choose to make our day about others and not about ourselves. May we not harbor bitterness or bring up past hurts against each other. May we lift up our wickedness and our weaknesses in confession to You. May we both live in obedience to You.

Lord, I pray over our knees today. We bow them to You and submit today. We submit to You, Your plan, and Your ways. May we willingly do so today.

Lord, I pray over our hands and feet today. May they be swift to serve and to do for others today. May we serve each other well today. Show us little ways and big ways that we can make a difference in this day.

Lord, as a husband today, You have called me to be the leader of this home. I pray that you would give me the wisdom that I need to lead this home for your glory. I need wisdom to understand my wife. Please help me to understand her as well as be able to adequately communicate with her. I also pray a hedge of protection around our marriage. Protect us, Lord, from the devil, the flesh, and the world. May our marriage be strengthened by You and be pleasing to You this day.

Write out your own prayers about being the spouse God wants you to be.

Praying God's Word Over Your Marriage

Matthew 19:4-6 "And he answered and said unto them, Have ye not read, that he which made them at the beginning made them male and female, and said, For this cause shall a man leave father and mother, and shall cleave to his wife: and they twain shall be one flesh? Wherefore they are no more twain, but one flesh. What therefore God hath joined together, let not man put asunder."

Lord, You have made my wife for me. May we be one. May we approach problems as one, face life as one, raise kids as one, and take care of our elderly parents as one. May no person on this earth put our marriage asunder. May we not allow our children, our parents, our coworkers, or our friends or family members, to pit us against each other. We are on the same team and we are one in Your sight. Help us to live life on the same team always working together and not against one another. I ask You to stop any person who wants to harm this marriage in the name of Jesus.

Joshua 1:9 "Have not I commanded thee? Be strong and of a good courage, be not afraid, neither be thou dismayed: for the LORD thy God is with thee whithersoever thou goest."

Lord, I pray your courage and strength as a husband and a wife. Our marriage will take us to some scary places and we will face some scary things, but may we have a courage to face what it is that will be in our future side by side with You before us.

Psalm 1:1-3 "Blessed is the man that walketh not in the counsel of the ungodly, nor standeth in the way of sinners, nor sitteth in the seat of the scornful. But his delight is in the law of the LORD; and in his law doth he meditate day and night. And he shall be like a tree planted by the rivers of water, that bringeth forth fruit in his season, his leaf also shall not wither; and whatsoever he doeth shall prosper."

Lord, I want my marriage to prosper. I want it to be faithful, fruitful and flourishing. In order for it to do that my wife and I must seek godly counsel. I pray we would do so. Surround us with godly influences and the guidance from the Spirit within us to make right choices and decisions. We need your help and your wisdom.

Psalm 37:3 "Trust in the LORD, and do good; so shalt thou dwell in the land, and verily thou shalt be fed."

Lord, help us to trust You and to do the works You have for us to do in our home and outside of our home. I ask for you to provide for our needs as a family. Thank You for Your faithfulness.

Psalm 37:4-5 "Delight thyself also in the LORD; and he shall give thee the desires of thine heart. Commit thy way unto the LORD; trust also in him, and he shall bring it to pass."

Lord, I pray that my wife and I delight in You. May we be committed unto You and commit our way to You. You will bring to pass what we are praying for in Your time and in

Your will and way. If the answer is "no" then that is for the best.

Psalm 51:10 "Create in me a clean heart, O God; and renew a right spirit within me."

Lord, may my heart be clean and may my wife's heart be clean before You. May we be right in Your sight, holy and acceptable. May we have a right spirit with You and with one another. A clean heart and a right spirit cannot be filled with selfishness or anger. I pray and confess anything that is hindering my right spirit and a clean heart.

Proverbs 24:3-4 "Through wisdom is an house builded; and by understanding it is established: And by knowledge shall the chambers be filled with all precious and pleasant riches."

Lord, I ask that you would give my wife and I wisdom and knowledge in how we should love one another. Help us to know how to please one another and to see the little things each day that would bless and help the other one. May everything we do, every choice we make, every action build this home and not tear it down. I ask that You would give us the knowledge we need so that the rooms of our home would be filled with precious and pleasant riches. Fill these rooms with laughter. Help us to enjoy one another and to have fun. Help us to view one another as precious and not to place our value on things or material possessions. May I view my wife a precious and may she view me the same way. Fill our home with precious joy and contentment, I pray.

Ecclesiastes 4:9-10 "Two are better than one; because they have a good reward for their labour. For if they fall, the one will lift up his fellow: but woe to him that is alone when he falleth; for he hath not another to help him up."

Lord, help me to be my wife's biggest fan and help her to be mine. Help us to lift each other up in prayer and in practical ways each day. May I give my wife the love she needs, and may she provide for me the respect my heart desires.

Song of Solomon 4:10 "How fair is thy love, my sister, my spouse! How much better is thy love than wine! And the smell of thine ointments than all spices!"

Lord, help me to treasure my wife daily.

Romans 15:5-6 "Now the God of patience and consolation grant you to be likeminded one toward another according to Christ Jesus: That ye may with one mind and one mouth glorify God, even the Father of our Lord Jesus Christ."

Lord, please grant us a like-mindedness in our home. May my wife and I have one mind, one mouth, and one purpose in this life – to glorify You. Help us to see things from each other's perspective and to understand one another. Guard us against drifting apart and from the plans of the evil one.

1 Corinthians 13:4-8 "Charity suffereth long, and is kind; charity envieth not; charity vaunteth not itself, is not puffed up, Doth not behave itself unseemly, seeketh not her own, is not easily provoked, thinketh no evil, Rejoiceth not in iniquity, but rejoiceth in the truth; Beareth all things, believeth all things, hopeth all things, endureth all things. Charity never fails..."

Lord, help my love to my spouse to be true love. True love is patient. True love envies not. True love isn't about me or mine at all. True love doesn't think, feel, say, or do unseemly things. True love doesn't lose its temper. True love doesn't think evil or stew about disappointments or arguments. True love puts up with the shortcomings of others and endures through it all. True love never fails. Help me to have this kind of love for my spouse and for her to have that same love for me. Help me to love her as You love Your bride, the Church.

Galatians 5:22-23 "But the fruit of the Spirit is love, joy, peace, longsuffering, gentleness, goodness, faith, Meekness, temperance: against such there is no law."

Lord, help me and my wife to each be filled with love – love for You and love for others. May we be filled with joy that isn't tied to circumstances but that is constant no matter what. May we be filled with Your peace even during the trying times. Help us to be patient with one another and with situations. May we be gentle with each other and careful of the other one's feelings. Help us to be good and to do good for others. May we be faith filled, trusting in You at all times. Help us to me meek and keep the stronghold of pride out of our hearts and minds. May we have self-control in every area of our lives.

Philippians 2:3-8 "Let nothing be done through strife or vainglory; but in lowliness of mind let each esteem other better than themselves. Look not every man on his own things, but every man also on the things of others. Let this mind be in you, which was also in Christ Jesus: Who, being

in the form of God, thought it not robbery to be equal with God: But made himself of no reputation and took upon him the form of a servant, and was made in the likeness of men: And being found in fashion as a man, he humbled himself, and became obedient unto death, even the death of the cross."

Lord, when there is strife in my home it is because there is sin in my home. Strife is born out of selfishness. I am a selfish person and that is sin. I confess it and rebuke that spirit of selfishness in the name of Jesus. I ask that You would remake me to be like You, selfless, giving, serving, and sacrificing. Cause me to see what the needs of others are and not to selfishly demand or expect them to serve me. Make me a servant, Lord. Make me like You.

Write out your own prayers, requests, and verses for your marriage.

____

____

____

____

____

____

Prayers for your Children

Praying God's Word Over Your Children

Psalm 127:3 "Lo, children are an heritage of the LORD: and the fruit of the womb is his reward."

Lord, thank you for my children. Thank you for who they are and the way You created them. They are precious gifts to me. Thank You for entrusting me with them. May I be the father to them You want me to be. My I lead them by my words and actions to have a heart for You. May I demonstrate an example of a godly earthly father because this will effect their view of You, the Heavenly Father.

2 Timothy 1:12b "…for I know whom I have believed, and am persuaded that he is able to keep that which I have committed unto him against that day."

Lord, I believe that only You can keep my children against all the "that days" that will come against them. Those "that days" are all my worst fears concerning my children. I cannot keep my children when these things happen, but You can. If I find myself trying to fix everything, manipulating, or trying to control, then I am believing that I am able and not You. Keep my kids, Lord. I commit them to You. I am persuaded that YOU are able to take care of my children.

Romans 10:9 – "That if thou shalt confess with thy mouth the Lord Jesus and shalt believe in thine heart that God hath raised him from the dead, thou shalt be saved."

Lord, my child needs you to redeem them. They are a sinner. May they confess with their mouth and believe in their heart Jesus died to save them. Convict my child, Lord, and show them they need to be saved.

Isaiah 49:25b "... for I will contend with him that contendeth with thee, and I will save thy children."

Lord, Satan wants my kids. Contend with him. Fight him. Protect them, I pray. There are plans the enemy has for my children. Thwart them. I pray You would keep them from the evil influences that he will cause to cross their path. Protect their minds from wrong thoughts, their eyes from seeing wicked things, their ears from Satanic lies, their mouth from speaking evil, and their heart from wayward emotions. Cause them to be quick to use their hands and feet for good to serve You and to do good for others. I pray for their knees. May they submit to earthly authority beginning with their parents and ultimately to You. Guard them from a rebellious heart, I pray.

Isaiah 54:13 "And all thy children shall be taught of the LORD; and great shall be the peace of thy children."

Lord, teach my children. Lord, may they be teachable. May they be humble and receive the instruction quickly and easily. Guard them from stubbornness and from a "know it all" attitude.

John 15:4-5 "Abide in me, and I in you. As the branch cannot bear fruit of itself, except it abide in the vine; no more can ye, except ye abide in me. I am the vine, ye are the branches: He that abideth in me and I in him, the

same bringeth forth much fruit; for without me ye can do nothing."

Lord, may my children, once saved, abide in You. May they not wander like the prodigal son. May they stay and abide in the safety and blessing of Your love and protection. May they bear much fruit for You. May they have a burden for lost souls and may they bring many people to You through a bold and effective witness. Give them boldness to stand for what is right in a very dark world.

Mark 12:30-31 "And thou shalt love the Lord thy God with all thy heart, and with all thy soul, and with all thy mind, and with all thy strength: this is the first commandment. And the second is like, namely this, Thou shalt love thy neighbor as thyself. There is none other commandment greater than these."

Lord, may my children love You with all their heart, soul, mind, and strength. May they see parents that do the same. May they always see You through a clear lens of love and goodness. May they not view You through a distorted lens of hurt and hate when things go wrong in their life. May they always be assured of Your love and Your goodness, I pray. Guard them from the many things that will vie for their heart's affection. Give them a heart for You and for others. May they love others and serve them. Give them compassion and a servant's heart, I pray.

Romans 8:31b "...If God be for us, who can be against us?"

Lord, may my children always know and believe that You are FOR them. I pray that You would stand against all of those forces of evil that will come against my children.

Romans 8:37 "Nay, in all these things we are more than conquerors through him that loved us."

Lord, I pray victory over my children. I pray you would help us, as parents, to see their strongholds and help them with them. I pray they would see them and not just live in their weakness and hide behind excuses or laziness. Make them more than conquerors, I pray. Give them a conquering attitude, mindset, and ability.

Joshua 1:9 "Have not I commanded thee? Be strong and of a good courage; be not afraid, neither be thou dismayed: for the LORD thy God is with thee whithersoever thou goest."

Lord, I pray my children would be strong in You. Give them courage, Lord. May they not be crippled by fear or anxiety. May they always know and be assured of Your presence in their life.

Psalm 139:7-10 "Whither shall I go from thy spirit? Or whither shall I flee from thy presence? If I ascend up into heaven, thou art there: if I make my bed in hell, behold, thou art there. If I take the wings of the morning, and dwell in the uttermost parts of the sea; Even there shall thy hand lead me, and thy right hand shall hold me."

Lord, I cannot be with my children every minute. They will be exposed to temptations and dangers. They will make wrong choices and they will be around people who want to bring them down. Lord, You can be with them at all times and You will be with them at all times. Cause them to know this and be fully aware that You see them and know what they are doing. Bring to mind truths from Your word when they are tempted. Stop the ones who want to bring them harm. Thank You for being with my children every moment of every day.

Ephesians 4:32 "And be ye kind one to another, tenderhearted, forgiving one another, even as God for Christ's sake hath forgiven you."

Lord, help my children to be kind people. Give them tender hearts. May they not be selfish and self-centered, hard hearted, and cruel. When people do them wrong, may they be forgiving just as You are to them.

2 Timothy 2:26a "And that they may recover themselves out of the snare of the devil..."

Lord, open my children's eyes to the lies and deceit that Satan is so very good at. May they not fall for the traps he will lay for them. Give them a wisdom and discernment that can only come from You, I pray.

Luke 2:52 "And Jesus increased in wisdom and stature, and in favour with God and man."

Lord Jesus, may my kids be just like You were when You were a child on this earth. As they grow, grow them in wisdom. Give them wisdom beyond their years, I ask. May they have favor with You and with man.

Psalm 119:133 "Order my steps in thy word: and let not any iniquity have dominion over me."

Lord, order my child's steps in Your word. Make their paths clear. Make the decisions they make plain before their eyes. May their career path be crystal clear to them and to us. May their choice of a future mate be made plain. Order their steps, Lord, and may they walk in obedience to You. Break the dominion sin has over them and may they walk in victory.

2 Corinthians 9:7b "...so let him give, not grudgingly, or of necessity: for God loveth a cheerful giver."

Lord, give my child a generous nature and heart. May they not be selfish and greedy. May they be givers and not takers, I pray.

1 Thessalonians 4:4 "That every one of you should know how to possess his vessel in sanctification and honour." 1 Corinthians 6:18 "Flee fornication. Every sin that man doeth is without the body; but he that committeth fornication sinneth against his own body."

Lord, I pray for my child sexually. Protect them from predators and those that would lure them into sex outside of marriage. May they grow up with this as their conviction not just ours. Give them the desire and commitment to stay pure until marriage. Help us to know how to talk openly to them about the dangers of sex outside of marriage and the wonders of sex as You designed it for marriage. I pray one day they would stand at that marriage altar pure and that the one they marry would do the same.

John 10:10 "The thief cometh not, but for to steal and to kill, and to destroy: I am come that they might have life, and that they might have it more abundantly."

Lord, Satan wants to steal everything You have promised from my children. He wants to destroy them. I pray they would not fall prey to his plans. I pray they would live in You to the fullest. May they have the life that You plan for them. May they live an abundant life.

Philippians 3:13b "...forgetting those things which are behind, and reaching forth unto those things which are before."

Lord, my child will encounter hardship and pain. May they not get stuck there. May they let it go and move forward.

Philippians 2:14 "Do all things without murmurings and disputings."

Lord, help my children with the battle of their tongue. May they speak respectfully to us and to others. May they not whine and complain or yell and argue. Help us not to accept anything less than complete obedience with respectful words.

Ephesians 6:1-4 "Children, obey your parents in the Lord: for this is right. Honour thy father and mother which is the first commandment with promise: That it may be well with thee and that thou mayest live long on the earth. And ye fathers, provoke not your children to wrath: but bring them up in the nurture and admonition of the Lord."

Lord, I pray that my children would be obedient and have submissive spirits. Guard them from the spirit of rebellion that is as witchcraft in your eyes. Help them to obey immediately and sweetly. Help us not to settle for less. May they honor us as their parents. I pray for respectful attitudes and for godly obedience. I want it to go well for my child and in order for it to be that way they must obey and honor. Help us not to provoke them and to know what battles we need to fight. Give us wisdom, I pray.

Isaiah 54:17 "No weapon that is formed against thee shall prosper; and every tongue that shall rise against thee in judgment thou shalt condemn. This is the heritage of the servants of the LORD, and their righteousness is of me, saith the LORD."

I pray this verse over my children in the name of Jesus. May no weapon against them human or satanic prosper. May every tongue that speaks against them falsely be silenced. This is their heritage, may they live in it fully.

2 Corinthians 10:4-5 "(For the weapons of our warfare are not carnal, but mighty through God to the pulling down of strongholds;) Casting down imaginations, and every high thing that exalteth itself against the knowledge of God, and bringing into captivity every thought to the obedience of Christ."

Lord, I pray we would wield the mighty weapons You have given us to pull down the strongholds in our home, in us personally, and that our children would do the same themselves. May we kick out every thought that exalts itself against Your truth. May every thought be brought into captivity and made to bow to You in obedience and complete surrender.

1 Corinthians 2:16b "...But we have the mind of Christ." *Lord, touch my child's mind. Help them in school or at work to understand and to try their best. Help them to know how to solve the problems that they face. Give them the creativity and ingenuity they need. Help them to know how You think about things and Your thoughts on the matter.*

Daniel 1:17b "God gave them knowledge and skill in all learning and wisdom..."

Lord, help my child in school or at work. Give them the ability they need to understand and excel in learning and wisdom.

Isaiah 30:21 "And thine ears shall hear a word behind thee, saying, This is the way, walk ye in it, when ye turn to the right hand and when ye turn to the left." *Lord, give my children ears to hear Your still small voice telling them which way they should go.*

Colossians 1:9-10 "For this cause we also, since the day we heard it, do not cease to pray for you, and to desire that ye might be filled with the knowledge of his will in all wisdom and spiritual understanding; That ye might walk worthy of the Lord unto all pleasing, being fruitful in every good work, and increasing in the knowledge of God."

Lord, fill my children with the knowledge of Your will. Give them all wisdom and spiritual understanding. Help them to walk worthy of You and to be pleasing and fruitful in every good work. May they be always increasing in the knowledge of God.

Colossians 3:15c "...and be ye thankful."

Lord, may my children not be demanding, greedy, ungrateful children. May they have a thankful and grateful heart.

Romans 4:20-21 "He staggered not at the promise of God through unbelief; but was strong in faith, giving glory to God; And being fully persuaded that, what he had promised, he was able also to perform."

Lord, when my children receive a promise from You, help them not to stagger at it or waver. May their belief and faith give You glory. May they be fully persuaded about Your power and Your person. May they rest assured that You will keep Your promises.

Write out your own prayers, requests, and verses for your children.

____

____

____

____

____

____

Ministry Prayers

Praying God's Word over your ministry

Isaiah 54:17 "No weapon that is formed against thee shall prosper; and every tongue that shall rise against thee in judgment thou shalt condemn. This is the heritage of the servants of the LORD, and their righteousness is of me, saith the LORD."

Lord, Satan has weapons formed against us in this ministry. He has people he will use. They will say things against us. They will lie about us, slander us, and will hurt us many times over. But I am asking for You to cause these people, their plans, and their painful words not to prosper. This is our heritage as Your servants. This is not about us, it is about You. They are not attacking us, they are attacking You. This is not our work, it is Yours. I stand in this heritage that we have today, and we ask for You to stop these weapons that are against us.

Isaiah 49:25b "... for I will contend with him that contendeth with thee..."

Lord, contend with the enemy when he comes against us in this ministry. When he uses people to come against us, contend with them, Lord. Fight for us, Lord. We need You to go to battle for us when the battle rages in our ministry.

1 Thessalonians 3:12 "And the Lord make you to increase and abound in love one toward another, and toward all men, even as we do toward you."

Lord, I ask that you help us to abound in love toward each other and toward all the people in the ministry we have. Give us a heart for them and fill us with love, compassion, and genuine care and concern for them.

1 Kings 3:9a "Give therefore thy servant an understanding heart to judge thy people that I may discern between good and bad..."

Lord, I pray that you would give us an understanding heart. Give us wisdom and discernment that can only come from You. Help us to make wise judgements and to know right from wrong and good from bad as we lead in our ministries.

Isaiah 11:2-4a "And the spirit of the LORD shall rest upon him, the spirit of wisdom and understanding the spirit of counsel and might, the spirit of knowledge and of the fear of the LORD; And shall make him of quick understanding in the fear of the LORD: and he shall not judge after the sight of his eyes, neither reprove after the hearing of his ears: But with righteousness shall he judge..."

Lord, I pray these verses over my life. May the spirit of the Lord rest upon me. May the spirit of wisdom and understanding fill me as I serve in this ministry. Help me to know how to structure, lead, and run this ministry. Give me that spirit of counsel, Lord. When people come to me, help me to know how to help them and give me the words to say to them. Lord, give me the spirit of might. Help me to have the strength and the energy I need to do what You have called me to do. Help me to sleep well so that I can wake up refreshed and reenergized and ready to face the day before me. Grant me knowledge and the know how to carry out the tasks before me. Fill me. Lead me. Guide me. Give me wisdom and discernment. May I fear you and be filled with quick understanding. Divinely enable and supernaturally empower me to fulfill the calling You have placed upon my life.

Daniel 9:22b "…I am now come forth to give thee skill and understanding."

Lord, I pray you would equip us with the skill and understanding we need in our ministries. Help us to be able to know how to proceed, organize, plan, lead, help, minister, and serve in these ministries.

1 Thessalonians 2:8 "So being affectionately desirous of you, we were willing to have imparted unto you, not the gospel of God only, but also our own souls, because ye were dear unto us."

Lord, help us to love people. Even when they are hard to love. Even when we are tired. Even when we are hurt or frustrated. Help us to love people and not to try to minister out of duty but out of devotion. May we not just share the gospel but share our own souls with people. That is what will make us real and will draw people to you.

Isaiah 50:4 "The LORD GOD hath given me the tongue of the learned, that I should know how to speak a word in season to him that is weary: he wakeneth morning by morning, he wakeneth mine ear to hear as the learned."

Lord, please help us to have the ear of the learned each morning. Help us to learn from You, to understand Your Word, and to then have the tongue of the learned. Help us to know how to speak a word to him or her that is weary. Give us wisdom in talking, counseling, teaching, and preaching. We need You to give us a learned ear and tongue.

Jeremiah 1:9 "Then the LORD put forth his hand, and touched my mouth. And the LORD said unto me, Behold I have put my words in thy mouth."

Lord, my words can do nothing to help another person. But if the words are Yours, they can make all the difference. Put Your words in my mouth, Lord. Put Your words in my husband's mouth. Help us as we teach, preach, counsel, or just have a conversation. Give us Your words.

1 Thessalonians 2:4 "But as we were allowed of God to be put in trust with the gospel, even so we speak; not as pleasing men, but God, which trieth our hearts."

Lord, sharing the gospel is a sacred gift and calling. In my weaknesses I can tend to be a people pleaser. I do not want people to dislike me. Help me to speak the truth to people and to say what will please YOU and not them. Help me not to feel the pressure to be liked or accepted by others. May I keep my goal and my sights on pleasing You and making You proud. Others will dislike me and even come against me. But as long as I please You, that is all that matters. Help this truth to be real to me each and every day.

Ephesians 6:5-7 "Servants, be obedient to them that are your masters according to the flesh, with fear and trembling, in singleness of your heart, as unto Christ; Not with eyeservice, as menpleasers; but as servants of Christ,

doing the will of God from the heart. With good will doing service, as to the Lord, and not to men."

Lord, You know my nature. Help my wife and I to get under what we need to get under so we can be over what we need to be over. We will not be effective leaders until we are obedient followers. Give us humility and a servant's heart. Help us to do everything we do as unto You and not to be seen of men. May Your opinion be most important to us. Help me not to be a performance driven Christian. Help me not to do what I do out of duty. May I serve and serve well for YOU.

Philippians 1:9-11 "And this I pray, that your love may abound yet more and more in knowledge and in all judgment; That ye may approve things that are excellent; that ye may be sincere and without offence till the day of Christ; Being filled with the fruits of righteousness, which are by Jesus Christ, unto the glory and praise of God."

Lord, I pray you would help us to abound more and more in knowledge and judgment. Help us to approve those things that are excellent in marriage, parenting, and ministering. Help us to be sincere. May we not offend, even when we speak the truth in love.

1 Peter 4:1 "If any man speak, let him speak as the oracles of God, if any man minister, let him do it as of the ability which God giveth: that God in all things may be glorified through Jesus Christ, to whom be praise and dominion for ever and ever. Amen."

Lord, there have been times when I have served and ministered for my own glory. I have ministered in my own ability and talent and it is exhausting and frustrating. It is unfruitful and disobedient. Help me to minister with the ability YOU give. May YOU be glorified in every action, attitude, act of service, and ministry I am involved in.

Ephesians 6:19 "And for me, that utterance may be given unto me, that I may open my mouth boldly, to make known the mystery of the gospel."

Lord, help me to boldly share the gospel. Help me to share it clearly without apology. Help me to have opportunities to witness publicly, privately, and personally.

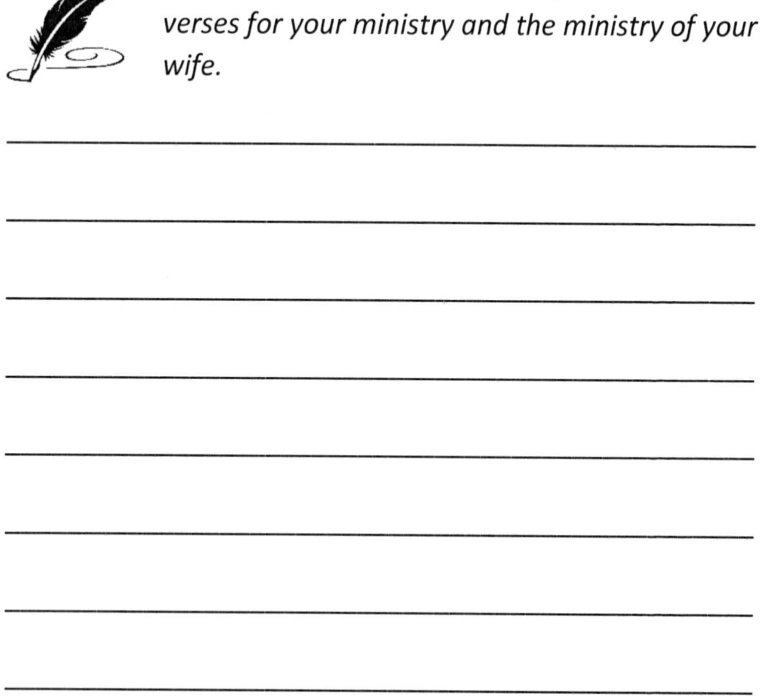

Write out your own prayers, requests, and verses for your ministry and the ministry of your wife.

Prayers for Others

Others

Galatians 6:2 "Bear ye one another's burdens, and so fulfil the law of Christ."

Colossians 1:3 "We give thanks to God and the Father of our Lord Jesus Christ, praying always for you."

Ephesians 6:18 "Praying always with all prayer and supplication in the Spirit, and watching thereunto with all perseverance and supplication for all saints."

Lord, there are so many around me with so many needs. People are hurting and people are struggling. Please help me not to be an island unto myself. Help me to care. Help me to lift people up in prayer each and every day. Help me to pray for others the way I hope others will pray for me when I am the one in need.

Write out requests, verses, and prayers for others.

____

____

____

____

____

Preaching Series

by Dr. Mike Edwards

Having a Godly Home in a X-Rat...
$10.00

Heaven: Surprising Truths About...
$10.00

The Book of Daniel
$10.00

What Every Christian Needs to K...
$10.00

Having Hope in Hopeless Times

JOSHUA, The Book of Victory

JUDGES, The Crumbling of a Nat...

Lessons From The Life of Lazarrus

Living with Confidence in a Chaot...
$10.00

NEHEMIAH, Let's Rise Up and B...
$10.00

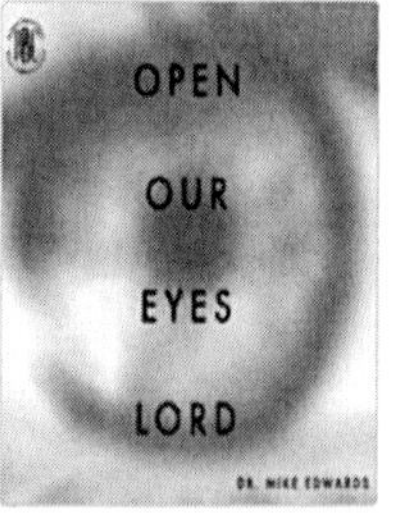

Open Our Eyes Lord
$10.00

RUTH, A Journey to Bethlehem
$10.00

Revelation - Vol 1

Revelation - Vol 2

Revival For Survival

Hope For The Hopeless

Marriage

By: Dr. Michael Edwards & Amy Edwards

Strengthening The Knot Marriage...

This Marriage Bundle includes an Audio Cd of Mrs. Amy Edward's Lesson "Communication Manual: Wife Edition" along with a lesson booklet and an Audio CD of Dr. Michael Edward's Lesson "A Biblical Blueprint of a Godly Husband" along with a lesson booklet. These are the Lessons that were taught at "The Strengthening The Knot Marriage Conference."

In this little 90 page book, I discuss times when you may find the joy of serving Jesus missing and what you can do to regain this precious joy.

Women of the Word ~ By Amy Edwards

Volume 1	Volume 2	Volume 3
308 pages	243 pages	301 Pages
Spiral Ring	Spiral Ring	Spiral Ring

Three books on the women of the Bible from A – Z. Spiral rings allow for easy journaling and note taking.

The Princess Project
By Amy Edwards

The Princess Project is a unique and interactive mother/daughter Bible study that uses the original Princess stories written by the brothers Grimm to teach timeless Scriptural truths. For each princess you will find a devotional for the mother and one for the daughter. 78 page spiral bound book.

Reflections ~ By Amy Edwards

Reflections is a yearlong daily journey through the Scriptures. By the end of this 4 volume series you will have read the entire Bible through and the books of Psalms and Proverbs twice. Each day has the daily reading assignments for you to read and a thoughtful provoking devotional written especially for women concerning the battles we face each and every day.

Vol. 1 – 278 pages

Vol. 2 – 294 pages

Vol. 3 – 279 pages

Vol. 4 – 377 pages

PBC Publications is audio sermons and books by Dr. Mike Edwards and Mrs. Amy Edwards.

You can have these items shipped to you or you can arrange to pick them up at PBC.

Please visit our website to purchase these and other publications at:
www.pbckannapolis.org